Christian Married Love

Christian Married Love

A Catholic Program for Marriage Preparation
Engaged Couple's Handbook

Fred and Lisa Everett

Our Sunday Visitor Publishing Division
Our Sunday Visitor, Inc.
Huntington, Indiana 46750

Imprimatur: ✠John Michael D'Arcy, S.T.D.
Bishop, Diocese of Fort Wayne-South Bend
June 10, 1993

The Imprimatur is an official declaration that a book or pamphlet is free of doctrinal or moral error. No implication is contained therein that those who grant an imprimatur agree with the contents, opinions, or statements expressed.

Scripture citations in this work are taken from the *New American Bible* © 1991, 1986, 1970 by the Confraternity of Christian Doctrine, Washington, D.C. All rights reserved. Original copyright © 1993 by Frederick Everett and Lisa Everett, Office of Family Life, Diocese of Fort Wayne-South Bend, Fort Wayne, IN 46801.

Copyright © 1997 by Our Sunday Visitor Publishing Division
Our Sunday Visitor, Inc.

All rights reserved. With the exception of short excerpts for critical reviews, no part of this book may be used or reproduced in any manner whatsoever without permission in writing from the publisher. Write:

Our Sunday Visitor Publishing Division
Our Sunday Visitor, Inc.
200 Noll Plaza
Huntington, IN 46750

International Standard Book Number: 0-87973-111-7

Cover design by Peggy Gerardot

Printed in the United States of America

Table of Contents

Foreword by Bishop John M. D'Arcy 7

Introduction 8

Chapter One
The Meaning of Married Love 9

Chapter Two
Challenges to Married Love 13

Chapter Three
Communication and Intimacy in Marriage 17

Chapter Four
Roles and Responsibilities in Marriage 21

Chapter Five
The Gift of Sexuality 25

Chapter Six
The Gift of Children 29

Chapter Seven
Christian Marriage as a Sacrament 33

Chapter Eight
The Christian Family as the Church of the Home 37

FOREWORD

As you approach one of the most significant days of your life, your heart is touched with hope and great expectations, but also, probably, with a little anxiety. Such feelings are normal, especially before making such a serious commitment as giving yourself to another in marriage. I had the same feelings myself before making the commitment to live my life as a priest. Just as I was assisted by the Church in discerning my vocation, the Church has a solemn responsibility of assisting you before you commence on this great adventure.

Through this handbook prepared by Fred and Lisa Everett, it is our wish to share with you the meaning of this new life together. We want you to understand and reflect upon the responsibilities that you will be undertaking. The true meaning of married love is quite different from the love we often learn about in the media and in much of the culture of our times. It is God's plan for married love that is explained to you in these pages.

As you begin this period of preparation for the wonderful vocation of married love, I wish you every grace and blessing. Marriage and family life are the great schools of life and love. While your life together will, at times, involve difficulties, as every life does, it is my hope and the hope of the Church that it will be marked, above all, by joy. More than anything, I pray that in these days and the days to come you will seek the help of God, who alone can fulfill your deepest hopes for your life together.

Most Reverend John M. D'Arcy
Bishop, Diocese of Fort Wayne-South Bend

INTRODUCTION

So, you're going to get married. We can still remember the glad faces, the surprised faces, the ecstatic faces, and even some of the doubtful faces among our relatives and college friends at the news of our engagement. It was a heady time for both of us. We were taking a step and setting a course which would not only transform our futures, but would also have lasting effects on our family and friends.

You, too, have taken a step and set a course which will transform your future as well as have lasting effects on your family and friends. It couldn't be otherwise. To stand up before one's family and friends and pronounce words which bind for life is a pivotal act. Marriage is one of those definitive institutions by which civilizations either thrive or crumble. You will be contributing in no small way to the future of many people in our society. Just consider:

• For you personally, a solid marriage will be an opportunity for you to experience the happiness that comes from making a gift of yourself to another person.

• For your family and friends, a solid marriage is a sign that fidelity is possible and that love makes life meaningful.

• For your children, a solid marriage is the foundation for their security and identity as witnessed in the love that you have for them and for each other.

With these considerations in mind, we have prepared this handbook for you. It is offered as an assistance in this important time of preparation, where you have a chance to consider the step you have taken and to make any adjustments in the course you have set. This handbook is by no means exhaustive. It will not answer every question or concern. It is offered, most importantly, to help you think about and discuss issues that need to be dealt with before your wedding day. Today especially, couples need to make sure that they are committing themselves to the same thing, and this assurance can only come through honest dialogue. You need to talk everything out.

One of the things we talked about before our wedding day was the issue of our shared Catholic faith. We found that even though we were both Catholic, we had our differences. Deciding how to handle those differences was settled when we both agreed that we would seek to learn what the Church taught and to follow it, regardless of who ended up being "right." We did this as an expression of our belief that Christ speaks through those whom he has sent to lead us: the Holy Father and the bishops in communion with him. Especially in issues of marital morality, this has been a great assistance for us and can be for you, even if both of you do not share the Catholic faith.

Even so, while marriage is a serious enterprise and does entail great responsibilities, we all know it isn't just that. People usually don't flock to something simply to have great responsibilities placed upon them. That certainly wasn't our single motivation. Marriage, just as dating, is about funny glances, tender embraces, and lively conversations. Often its greatest joys are momentary and unexpected. Especially when children arrive, even a simple gesture or phrase can evoke a deep sense of intimacy or solidarity. Surely your journey together has already been touched by such moments. This period of preparation gives you the opportunity to set the foundation for many more.

So, good luck in the days ahead. We wish you a lifetime of happiness together.

Fred and Lisa Everett
Co-Directors, Office of Family Life
Diocese of Fort Wayne-South Bend

The Meaning of Married Love

Beloved, let us love one another, because love is of God.
—1 John 4:7

All people seek to find meaning and happiness in their lives. Deep in our hearts, most of us come to realize that to find this meaning and happiness, we must first encounter the gift of love and then make a sincere gift of ourselves for the good of others. Pope John Paul II has written that people cannot live without love and that our lives are senseless if we do not experience love and make it our own. This really is the great truth about who we are as men and women created in the image and likeness of God, who lives in himself a communion of love. Since we bear this divine image, each of us longs for personal friendship and communion with God and with others.

Even when we were children, we sensed that friendship was a special source of happiness. A good friend would be the one with whom we could share good times, but also times that were difficult. He or she would be the one who would stand by us if we were in trouble or if we were down. Such a person would show us the qualities of a true friend — qualities such as respect, generosity, patience, loyalty, sincerity, and understanding.

As we grew older, we discovered in ourselves an increased interest in members of the other sex. Suddenly, a world of dating and romance opened up a whole new horizon for forming friendships that would be more intimate than anything experienced previously and that one day could lead to marriage. Sometimes, the waiting was the most difficult part. Ultimately, we were waiting for someone who would be our best friend, someone who would show us all the qualities of a true friend, someone we could trust completely with our lives and with our future. We were waiting to encounter the gift of married love and to make a complete gift of ourselves to that special person someday.

Even so, married love is more than just a best friendship. It is more than the continuation of the romance. Married love is the fruit of an unconditional commitment to be love-giving and life-giving. As such, it has a certain meaning that God, in his wisdom and love, has intended according to his plan for marriage and the family. This meaning is well expressed in the intentions that a couple declares in the marriage liturgy just before they make their vows. They would be the positive responses made to these questions:

- Have you come here freely and without reservation to give yourselves to each other in marriage?

- Will you love and honor each other as man and wife for the rest of your lives?

• Will you accept children lovingly from God and bring them up according to the laws of Christ and his Church?

Married love, therefore, aims at a deeply personal unity. It is a love that is fully human and total, that is embraced freely and encompasses the whole person: body, mind, heart, and soul. It is a love that is faithful and exclusive, that is based on an unconditional commitment and lasts until death. It is a love that is fruitful, that welcomes children as gifts from God, and strives to raise them as his sons and daughters. Married love, ultimately, provides the proper foundation for that broader communion of love which is the family.

Questions for Reflection

1. How would you evaluate your own experiences of marriage and family life? What was positive? What was negative?

2. How have these experiences and your reflections on them shaped your expectations of marriage and family life?

3. How would you describe your friendship with your future spouse? Are you best friends? As a couple, do you share a common vision of marriage as a complete gift of self to one another for life?

Expectations

As you prepare for your married life together, you will probably realize that you have already formed some expectations about what that life together will mean. These expectations might be directly inherited from your own experiences of family life or derived from your own reflections or desires. Some of these expectations might deal with day-to-day activities such as who will mow the lawn or who will do the dishes. Others might have to do with larger issues such as how large a family to have or where to live. Great or small, these expectations will have an effect on the future happiness of your marriage and need to be expressed before the wedding day.

Today, because of the diversity of our cultural backgrounds and personal preferences, sharing and evaluating values and expectations together with your future spouse is especially important. Ignoring differences or downplaying their importance can be disastrous. Make sure to talk everything through.

The Right Attitude

> "Well, I probably intended to keep 'fooling around' when we got married."
> "I figured that if it didn't work out, we could split up."
> "We never seriously considered the possibility of having children."

The kind of statements made above can often be found in the case files of those petitioning for an "annulment" after a divorce. An annulment is simply a declaration by a proper authority that a marriage never existed. The above statements could have been made by either party and they serve as evidence that neither actually entered into a marriage. Why is this? Because one or both of them was not intending what it really means to get married, that is, to make a gift of self in a commitment that is exclusive, that lasts until death, and that is open to children. In other words, one or both of them did not have the right attitude.

Sharing the right attitude is crucial to the success of any marriage. Engaged couples need to take the time to look at the reasons why they are getting married. They need to recognize the mature decision to love unconditionally that is required by married love. Devices such as prenuptial agreements, which are contracts made before marriage that spell out how possessions should be divided in case of divorce, probably indicate either a lack of commitment or a lack of trust in the other party. Both commitment and trust are essential to the success of any marriage.

While all of us have been touched by the effects of divorce in one way or another, this is no reason to assume that your marriage has only a fifty-fifty chance of making it. Like anything in life, if we want to see good results, we have to make the necessary investment. Married love is not a fifty-fifty proposition: it requires both the husband and the wife to make a one hundred percent investment of self to be truly successful. Sharing the right attitude will go a long way in overcoming our personal failings and the difficulties which touch any family.

NOTES

Challenges to Married Love

Love is patient, love is kind. It is not jealous, [love] is not pompous, it is not inflated, it is not rude, it does not seek its own interests, it is not quick-tempered, it does not brood over injury, it does not rejoice over wrongdoings but rejoices with the truth. It bears all things, believes all things, hopes all things, endures all things.
—1 Corinthians 13:4-7

To love well is the work of a lifetime, and a great marriage is the fruit of a lifetime of work. When a man and a woman begin their lifelong journey together, they often are so enthusiastic and idealistic that they do not appreciate the challenges, both great and small, that await them. The small challenges, for example, can stem from such irritations as how the husband piles up his dirty clothes on a bedroom chair or how the wife splashes water all over the sink while washing her face. While small challenges such as these might occasion a rude remark or nagging, they present a husband and wife with ample opportunities to grow in patience and love. Many newly married couples, accustomed to the pleasant feelings associated with "being in love," are surprised to find that they sometimes have to make a conscious effort just to act in a civil and kind way toward their spouse in a given situation. Sometimes there are more serious challenges awaiting a newly-married couple. These challenges can come from the values which have formed our minds and hearts. They can arise from the destructive values present within our family or our culture which we have come to accept. Our Western culture, for example, stresses individualism, materialism, and pleasure-seeking. At times, we can be tempted to put ourselves or our own interests first and to avoid acquiring the self-giving attitudes which are at the heart of married love. Self-centered attitudes can lead a couple to be more concerned about material possessions than about the quality of their friendship or their own personal growth and maturity. They can lead a couple to seek their happiness in pleasurable activities and to avoid what is perceived as painful or burdensome. Such calculating attitudes can only lead to a shallow and short-lived contentment. Ultimately, the true happiness that married love brings can come only from the free gift of ourselves for the good of our husband or wife, no matter how hard it may seem in a given moment.

Our culture often challenges us with a false idea of freedom that claims that a person should be able to do whatever he or she wants to do, without regard for what is right or wrong or what is in the best interest of another person. Popular movies and television shows regularly glamorize the pursuit of power, wealth, and sexual pleasure at the expense of those personal values which bring true happiness. Those who are seduced by this idea of freedom shy away from the concept of sacrificial love and sometimes cynically mock the unconditional commitment of marriage. Ultimately, this false sense of freedom actually undermines the maturity needed to make and keep a serious commitment.

Only people who are sufficiently mature have the freedom to commit themselves to doing what is right and good in a particular situation, including marriage. They are able to be unselfish, to act in a loving way, and to be in control of their desires rather than being controlled by them. They are able to face, with confidence in God's assistance, both the daily challenges that inevitably come to every married couple and the difficult circumstances that may arise as the years go by.

Questions for Reflection

1. What challenges to having a happy marriage and family life do you perceive as present in our culture?

2. What challenges has your friendship faced already? What sacrifices have each of you been willing to make?

3. What attitudes have hurt your unity as a couple? What signs of maturity do you see in one another? Are there any warning signs in your relationship that you need to discuss together?

Warning Signs

While having the right attitude is a crucial first step in approaching marriage, there are still other factors which could indicate waiting a little longer or discussing certain issues more carefully. Often, there are warning signs that should indicate to a couple that certain issues should be resolved before a marriage can take place:

• If one or both are *teenagers*, issues that revolve around financial, emotional, and psychological readiness need to be addressed with the help of a professional counselor. Teenage marriages have a high incidence of divorce.

• If one or both have not sufficiently developed a *sense of identity*, of who they are and what their values are, they need to discuss whether they have developed their mind and heart well enough to actually give who they are to another.

• If one or both have a *drug or alcohol* dependency, or are children of parents with such dependencies, those issues need to be resolved with professional help.

• If the relationship has been *brief or imbalanced,* that is, if the engaged couple has not spent a sufficient time getting to know each other, then they should consider whether they should hold off the wedding until they have a better understanding of the other person's values, beliefs, attitudes, and habits.

• If one or both have experienced an *unhappy home life* or are trying to escape a situation at home, they should discuss this and consider if these circumstances might be having an undue influence on their decision to marry.

• If there is *parental pressure* to marry or not to marry, this is an issue that needs to be dealt with in a realistic manner since this can be particularly stressful.

• If both *family and cultural backgrounds* are very different, including differences in religious affiliation, these are issues that need to be discussed realistically since this can add a good deal of stress to a relationship.

• If the engaged couple is *sexually active,* then they may not have developed a strong relationship built upon mutual respect, responsibility, and communication. If so, the couple will need to assess the true strength of their friendship by adopting a chaste lifestyle for a period of time before actually getting married.

• If the engaged couple has gone a step further and they are *living together*, then they will have to consider whether they have really been able to develop a strong relationship. Studies have shown that cohabiting couples have a higher incidence of divorce and other marital problems than those who did not live together before marriage. A cohabiting couple that is sexually active should seriously consider living separately and chastely for a sufficient time during which they can better assess whether they really should get married.

• If the engaged couple is experiencing a *pregnancy,* they should seriously consider whether they really are ready to get married and whether the child should be placed for adoption.

NOTES

Communication and Intimacy in Marriage

So that they may all be one,
as you, Father are in me and I in you,
that they also may be in us,
that the world may believe that you sent me.
—John 17:21

Relationships — how do they grow? How does the personal friendship between a husband and a wife become deeper and stronger as the years go by, as it must if their marriage is to be happy and full of meaning? One of the essential ingredients in building this kind of relationship is communication, especially on matters important to the marriage and the family.

Communication about oneself and about one another's strengths, weaknesses, hopes, fears, joys, and sorrows is crucial to two people being able to know and accept each other as they really are. It is the foundation for emotional and spiritual intimacy in which two people share their inmost selves with one another. When this kind of communication, combined with expressions of tenderness and affection, is a part of daily life, then the relationship between a husband and wife becomes something of great depth, and their moments of sexual intimacy become a true expression of the self-giving love that is going on day in and day out. This is the kind of friendship for which every married couple hopes, and it begins with building communication and intimacy. All of us are aware that from time to time we place obstacles to good, in-depth communication. We may assume that, because the other person loves us, he or she will automatically know all of our needs. We may close up and not share with the other person what is really troubling us. Perhaps we do not listen: we are so anxious to say what is on our mind or to defend our point of view that we do not really hear and understand the concern or even the pain of the other person. We may choose inopportune times or inappropriate ways to express our frustrations. It may even happen that our schedules are so hectic that we simply do not set aside sufficient time to really talk to each other, one on one.

While obstacles such as these limit the effectiveness of communication in marriage, there is another kind of communication, a false and destructive communication, that can seriously harm a relationship. For example, when we are manipulative or abusive, when we talk down to the other person or try to dominate him or her, or when we are constantly nagging the other person, we weaken the relationship, and our words become weapons with which to fight instead of tools with which to build.

Even in the best of marriages, there will arise difficulties in communication and occasional disagreements. However, when both people are working hard every day to overcome these obstacles with respectful and honest dialogue, the quality of their married love becomes deeper, stronger, and more mature. Only this kind of love will provide the necessary foundation for the intimate partnership that marriage is meant to be.

Questions for Reflection

1. How do you express your love and respect for one another on a daily or weekly basis?

2. How has your communication grown since you first met? Are you able to share your deepest thoughts and feelings?

3. What obstacles to good communication have you encountered in your relationship? Are there topics you cannot discuss with each other? Has your communication ever been destructive?

Mixed Signals

> *Wife:* "Please, don't raise your voice!"
> *Husband:* "Look, that's the way I express myself when I get excited."

Communicating effectively is a skill that we all need to master. When we were children, it probably didn't take us long to realize that grunting in a general direction wasn't the most effective way to get something we wanted. We would learn in our homes that words like "please" and "thank you" were a part of communicating respectfully and effectively. Even so, while we may have learned over the years to communicate well within our own circle of family and friends, this is no guarantee that our future spouse will always understand what we are trying to express. Differences in your family or cultural backgrounds can at times be so great that learning effective communication may be the first order of business.

For example, a husband may come from a background where talking loudly and even yelling is commonplace. The wife, on the other hand, may come from a home where someone who is raising his or her voice must be very upset or angry. Consequently, when the husband raises his voice during an ordinary discussion, the wife can have a very negative reaction, even though the husband may not realize or intend the message his wife is receiving. What started as a simple discussion may end up as a furious fight. Couples need to understand and appreciate the differences in their family and cultural backgrounds in order to more effectively communicate. The repeated mixed signals from both verbal and non-verbal expressions can cause needless stresses in any marriage. If you simply make sure that you are sincerely and respectfully listening and expressing yourself, these types of problems will work themselves out over time.

Fighting Fair

Communication between a husband and wife will occasionally develop into an argument, perhaps involving an angry confrontation. This type of "fighting" does not necessarily mean that their communication was destructive. However, in order to prevent arguments from degenerating into destructive communication, consider the following tips for fighting fair:

• Stay focused on the issue at hand: don't bring up other problems or reopen previous arguments which have no bearing on the issue.

• Refrain from making accusations about each other's motives: discuss specific actions or behaviors that are bothering you.

• Avoid using emotional exaggerations like "always" and "never."

• Refrain from making personal attacks: emotional or physical abuse is always destructive and can only worsen the situation.

NOTES

Roles and Responsibilities in Marriage

There are different kinds of spiritual gifts but the same Spirit; there are different forms of service but the same Lord; there are different workings but the same God who produces all of them in everyone.
—1 Corinthians 12:4-6

Partnerships — we see many of them in everyday life: two or more people working together toward a common goal, each one bringing his or her gifts to a common endeavor. The marriage partnership, which the Church describes as "an intimate partnership of life and love," is one of a man and woman who are equal in dignity, though different in gifts and talents. Part of the process of preparing for this partnership involves recognizing and appreciating our own unique gifts so that we will be able to put these gifts at the service of our spouse and children. This will enable us to share responsibilities fairly and in a way that strengthens our marriage and family life.

First of all, men and women bring the gifts of their own masculinity and femininity to marriage and family life. While there may have been a tendency in previous generations to unfairly stereotype certain qualities or responsibilities as exclusively male or female, there are, nevertheless, natural differences between men and women which are meant to enrich their own relationship and to complement each other in caring for their children. Women, for example, tend to have a more complex emotional life than do men, are generally more aware of and responsive to concrete needs, and place great importance on personal relationships. As a wife and mother, a woman finds a unique fulfillment in fostering the development of the human person in all of its dimensions, especially through the experiences of bearing, nursing, and nurturing children. Men, on the other hand, tend to be more abstract and analytical than women, to experience a certain detachment from their bodies and emotions, and to place great importance on attaining goals and achieving success. As a husband and father, a man finds a unique fulfillment in ensuring the harmonious development of all the members of his family, providing for and protecting them. These are among the natural gifts that men and women bring to marriage and family life, and we find in this working complementarity the wise design of God himself.

In addition to these natural gifts, there are many acquired gifts which vary from couple to couple. For example, in some marriages today, it is the wife who, due to her education or expertise, manages the finances while the husband may be a gourmet chef. Since engaged couples sometimes approach marriage with the assumption that they and their future spouse will divide responsibilities in much the same way as did their own parents, it is important to discuss with each other on a regular or periodic basis what needs to be done in creating a home together, and to decide which spouse is best suited to which tasks. A couple should bring their own unique gifts and talents to their marriage for each other and eventually for their children. What arises from this mutual self-giving of a man and a woman is a dynamic and fruitful partnership which is an essential part of the plan of God for married love.

Questions for Reflection

1. What gifts do each of you bring to your relationship? How will they strengthen your partnership in marriage?

2. How do you envision your roles as husband and wife, mother and father? How will you share your responsibilities?

3. How will your work outside the home be at the service of your family life? How will you handle your money and material possessions with a sense of stewardship?

Working Hard

Most couples realize that a fulfilling marriage and family life require a good deal of hard work both at home as well as outside the home in order to provide for the family. Given our culture, the tendency seems to be to devote less time and focus to what needs to be done at home, at least with regard to interpersonal relationships, and to devote more to what needs to be done at "work." Sometimes, the balance may be so tipped that while a given spouse may think he or she is working for the good of the family, the reality is very different. We need to be conscious of our inclinations toward material values, often at the expense of interpersonal values. A father, for example, who works too many hours without real necessity allows his relationship with his wife or children to suffer. A mother who without necessity places her child in day care is depriving that child of the richness and warmth of her personal attention. All work should serve the good of the family.

Family Relations

Even in the most loving families, tensions between couples and in-laws are to be expected. Relationships between parents and their children are such that when their children marry, certain adjustments are inevitable. Engaged couples should remember that this is a new relationship coming into being and that they need to act as one: they need to be real partners. Parents and other relatives may at times be quick to offer their advice. This is normal and to be expected. Their advice, especially that of parents, should receive a respectful hearing. Even so, a couple should be wary of those who make unreasonable demands. Ultimately, it should always be the couple who come together to openly discuss their thoughts and feelings in determining a particular course of action. In this way, a solid foundation will be laid for their future years together as a couple, as a family, and as members of a wider circle of family and friends.

Finances

As in any partnership, good money management is an important factor in successfully maintaining a family. The bottom line is that a family's finances need to be handled responsibly, with a sense of stewardship, in order to provide for its needs. A sense of stewardship enables a couple to regard money and material possessions as gifts from God, entrusted to them for the common good, both of their family and of society as a whole. In order to do this effectively, a couple needs to discuss financial issues and to make a realistic budget so that their expenditures reflect the values of moderation and simplicity. While setting aside some money in savings is important, so is generosity in giving to the Church and other charitable organizations. In fact, the biblical practice of tithing, that is, giving a tenth of one's income, is still practiced by many as a concrete way of expressing their gratitude to God for all that he has given them.

Notes

The Gift of Sexuality

*That is why a man leaves his father and mother and
clings to his wife, and the two of them become one body.*
—Genesis 2:24

One of the greatest gifts that God gives to a married couple is the privilege and joy of expressing their love for one another by becoming "one body" in sexual union. While this union is meant to be both physically pleasurable and emotionally fulfilling, it is, above all, the deepest sign of the gift of self that a husband and wife make to each other on their wedding day.

According to God's design, this gift of two people in sexual union has two purposes: strengthening married love and sharing that love with children. As the most intimate sign by which each spouse makes a gift of himself or herself to the other and accepts his or her spouse as a gift, their sexual union is meant to express and to deepen the same self-giving love that each tries to show the other in their daily life together. When a husband and wife sincerely try to serve each other day in and day out, then the expression of their love in sexual union is the living out of a profound truth. Otherwise, their sexual union can simply become another means of gratifying their sexual desires rather than be an expression of giving themselves for the good of the other.

This is one of the reasons why couples are called by God to refrain from having sexual relations until marriage. To give my body to another person without first having given him or her my whole self in marriage, before God and before the community, would be to express through the "language" of the body a unity which does not yet exist. In other words, sexual union outside of marriage is actually a lie since the body is expressing a complete gift of self which really has not been made. In addition, a couple who is sexually involved before marriage usually will have skipped some of the steps that will make for a strong and mature relationship. Communication, personal intimacy, and understanding often suffer. Self-restraint, even if practiced only late in a relationship, will enable an engaged couple to come to the altar on their wedding day better prepared to give themselves to one another for life.

This mutual gift of self which is expressed in sexual union does not end with the couple, but rather makes them capable of the greatest possible gift: the gift by which they become co-creators with God in giving life to a new human person. This connection between the love-giving and life-giving purposes of sexual union is so close that it is impossible to truly have one without the other. This is why every act of sexual love must be open to life. To take a pill or to use some kind of device to avoid a pregnancy changes what a husband and wife are communicating to each other through the "language" of the body. Contraception and sterilization contradict the meaning of sexual union as a sign of total self-giving and openness to life. It is as if a man and a woman are saying, "I want you, but not all of you," or "I give myself to you, but not completely; I hold something back." For married love to be true to itself, there can be no holding back.

This does not mean that a couple should not plan their family, but rather, that the spacing or limiting of births should be done through a method of natural family planning, which respects the dignity of the human person and acknowledges fertility as a gift from God.

Questions for Reflection

1. What are your expectations of your sexual life together? How have you both been able to handle sexual feelings in your relationship? How do you show affection to one another?

2. Do you both share a vision of sexual intercourse as the expression of the complete gift of self that is made on your wedding day?

3. How will you be open to children in your sexual life? Are you both committed to expressing your sexuality in a healthy and moral way? Have you discussed natural family planning?

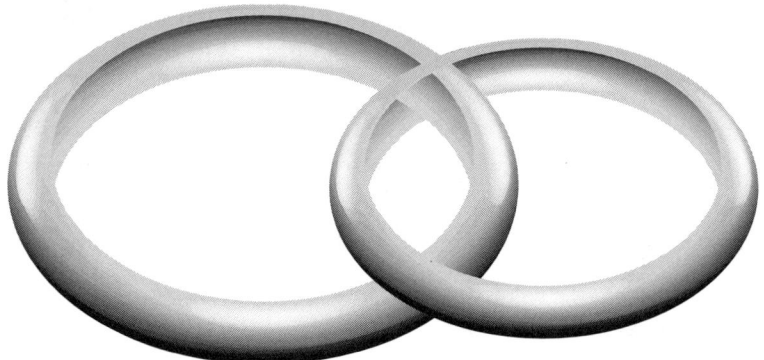

Good Sex

Anyone who has stood at a supermarket check-out counter knows that "good sex" is crucial to romance. The problem with the periodicals that one finds there is that they have no idea what "good sex" really means. It really has little to do with innovative techniques or positioning. It has much to do with respect, purity, tenderness, and, of course, the sweet passion that is found between lovers who in their hearts belong more to their beloved than to their very selves. Good sex does not have to do with maximizing physical pleasure, but with becoming one in body, mind, heart, and soul. This unity can only be accomplished by those acts which result in the natural union of man and woman as God intended. Other actions which result in physical pleasure, if they are not part of or do not lead to this natural union, only cheapen and degrade the physical expression of married love. The natural sexual union of husband and wife is a gift that gives glory to God, our Creator.

Planning a Family Naturally

Many couples associate effective family planning with pills and devices and consider natural family planning, if they have ever heard of it, as an unreliable method of birth control. However, modern methods of natural family planning have been shown in international studies to have an effectiveness rate of between 98 and 99 percent for couples who have been properly instructed. While the birth control pill has a comparable effectiveness rate, better than most other forms of artificial contraception, it also has side effects which can seriously endanger the health of the woman. The fact that birth control pills have negative health consequences should not be surprising considering that in taking synthetic hormones, a woman is actually introducing chemicals into her body for the purpose of upsetting its proper functioning. In other words, while authentic medicines act to restore the proper functioning of the body, the birth control pill when used as a contraceptive does just the opposite.

In addition, there is strong evidence that the newer forms of the birth control pill work not only by suppressing ovulation and therefore preventing conception, but they also make the woman's womb inhospitable to a newly conceived life, causing in some cases what is really an early abortion. When a couple considers these factors, it really does make sense to live in harmony with the way in which our bodies have been created. Just as we fault those who pollute the environment, we need also to respect the "ecology" of our own bodies.

Natural family planning does respect the "ecology" of our own bodies since it is based upon the natural cycle of fertility of the woman. A couple that has been properly instructed in natural family planning knows how either to achieve a pregnancy or to avoid one for a time. By observing the physical symptoms of ovulation, a couple can together pray and decide what God wants of them on a periodic basis. Consequently, natural family planning strengthens married love by fostering such qualities as communication, cooperation, mutual respect, and responsibility.

Notes

The Gift of Children

And whoever receives one child such as this in my name receives me.
—Matthew 18:5

Children are the supreme gift of marriage, the living reflection of the love between husband and wife. They come into the world completely dependent on their parents for food, clothing, shelter, and all the goods of this world. Most importantly, they depend on their parents for love. All of the research of recent decades confirms what we instinctively know: children will not be able to love others unless they have first been loved. So much depends on their being loved by their parents in order that they themselves might one day have the capacity to give themselves to others.

Studies on child development have shown that the most important characteristics and qualities that a person has as an adult are developed and formed while he or she is growing up in a family. A person's self-image, "Who am I?" and self-esteem, "Am I valuable; am I loveable; am I forgivable?" are formed, above all, within the family. A person's sense of morality, of right and wrong, is primarily developed during this time. It is in the family that a child first learns what it means to be loved unconditionally and what it means to love others in return. Even a child's first ideas of God depend upon his or her parents. We learn from the Scriptures that God is a Father, that he is caring and tender, that he never leaves us, that he is with us in the worst of times as well as in the good times, and that he forgives. He asks something of us for others as well as for our own benefit. Children will believe this about God if they have found it mirrored by their own parents. If we reflect on our own childhood experiences, we can easily see what an important impact our own parents have had on the way that we look at ourselves, our relationships with others, and even our relationship with God. For better or for worse, the home is a child's first and most important school. So great is the influence of the family in forming the kind of person that each of us becomes that Pope John Paul II has made this profound statement: "The future of humanity passes by way of the family."

As parents, we have the primary right and responsibility to educate our children. The most important aspect of this education involves guiding their spiritual, moral, and intellectual growth so that they might become men and women of faith who truly love God and who are capable of giving themselves in service to other people. What matters most in the eyes of God is not what kind of career or how many possessions our children will have, but rather, what kind of people they will become. Character formation is job one. What a tremendous responsibility this is, but what a great adventure as well.

Parents, however, are not just on the giving end of this relationship. Not only do children bring a great deal of joy to their parents, but parents often learn much about life and love from their children, even as they are trying to raise them. It has been said that in the early years after the first child has arrived, the parents are the ones who do most of the growing up. The countless demands that children make upon parents day and night, challenging though they may be, are some of the greatest opportunities we are given as human beings for growing in love. The desire to respond to our children's needs, to be good examples to them, and to pass on to them all those things which we have discovered to be true and good and beautiful is one of the strongest incentives that exists for sincerely striving to acquire in our own lives the virtues that will make us more mature and loving men and women.

Questions for Reflection

1. How do you feel about welcoming children generously? Have you both discussed when you want to start a family and how you will provide for your family's well-being?

2. As a couple, do you both share a vision of parents as the primary educators of their children? What values would you try to instill in them? What kind of persons would you want them to become?

3. How would you feel if the two of you were unable to have children of your own?

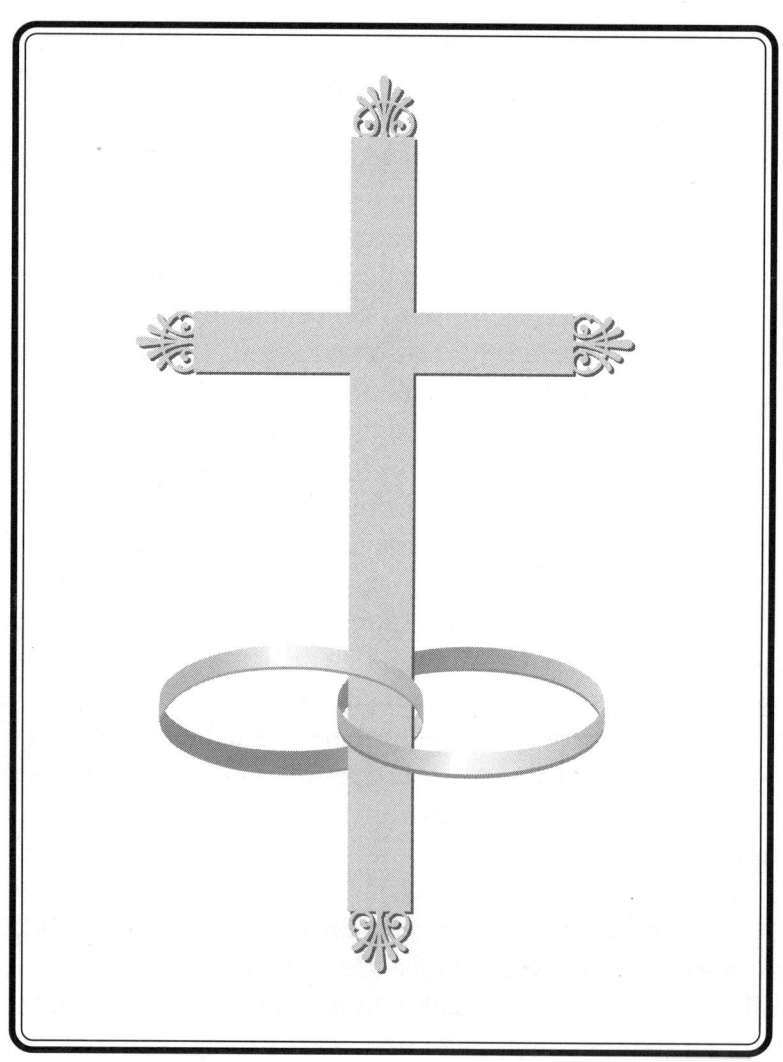

Becoming a Family

With the arrival of the first child, the communion of life and love that is a marriage becomes the foundation for a broader community — that of a family.

This transition usually entails a significant adjustment on the part of the new parents, who must now consider the needs of their child in their daily and long-term decisions. Some couples understandably fear that having a baby in the first few years of their married life will take time and energy away from getting to know and love each other better. This may be true in some cases, but if a couple's love for each other is sufficiently mature, parenthood will actually deepen their knowledge of and love for each other like no other shared experience can. Most couples are amazed at the depth of emotion and concern that this dependent and defenseless human being calls forth from them. It is a beautiful experience to see your husband or wife gradually grow into the role of a mother or father.

How Many?

When a couple decides to plan their family, the question of how many children to have naturally arises. In discussing this issue, a married couple should bear in mind that a central part of married love is an openness and generosity in the service of life. Certainly, a couple should avoid having so many children that they cannot properly care for them or give them adequate attention. This would not be in accordance with God's plan. On the other hand, there is the other extreme, one which is more common today, of automatically considering only one or two children. Married couples need to place priority on the personal values found in creating a community of love where children are welcomed as blessings from God, and are not seen as burdens to be avoided. In the final analysis, a couple needs to consider the good of their family, their society, and the Church in making a prayerful decision as to the number of children they will have.

Infertility

It is estimated that one in four married couples experiences problems with their fertility. These problems can range from a degree of difficulty in conceiving a child to not being able to have any children at all. For the infertile couple, the realization that they will never be able to conceive their own children or to have any more of their own can be a devastating blow. Periods of depression or low self-esteem can affect the infertile couple, especially if their infertility is related to their use of certain artificial contraceptives or the contraction of some sexually transmitted diseases. While this situation may cause great suffering, the couple's infertility does not make their marriage of any less value. Instead, a couple should approach their infertility as a call from God to express their openness and generosity in the service of life in other ways, perhaps by adopting children or helping in their parish family through teaching and community service.

NOTES

Christian Marriage as a Sacrament

This is my commandment: love one another as I love you.
No one has greater love than this, to lay down one's life for one's friends.
—John 15:12-13

A sacrament is a visible sign that points to and makes present an unseen reality. In the Sacrament of Baptism, for example, the pouring of or immersion in water symbolizes, among other things, a cleansing from sin, and this gesture, accompanied by the appropriate words, actually accomplishes such a spiritual cleansing and rebirth in Jesus Christ. When a baptized man and woman, whether Catholic, Protestant, or Orthodox, get married, they become the ministers of another sacrament, the Sacrament of Marriage. This sacrament is a sign of the covenant of love between Christ and his Church, and it actually gives the spouses the grace to love each other and their children as Christ loves us. When a baptized man and woman make a promise to one another on their wedding day, Christ, in turn, makes a promise to them. They promise to be true to one another in good times and in bad, in sickness and in health, and to love and honor each other all the days of their lives. And Christ promises to be with them in good times and in bad, in sickness and in health, and to give them the light and strength they need to love and honor each other all the days of their lives. In baptism, we were reborn in the image and likeness of Christ, the Son of God; in marriage, we become like Christ the Lover who gave his life for his beloved bride, the Church.

The Sacrament of Marriage gives us the privilege of participating in a love that is much greater than ourselves: the very love that led Christ to the cross. It is also a love that entrusts us with a mission to make present to one another, to our children, and to the world this very same love. This is the reason why a sacramental marriage is especially indissoluble: the covenant between a Christian husband and wife cannot be dissolved because it is a living sign of the love of God for his people. Christ is a faithful lover. He said to us, "I will never leave you." A husband and wife promise one another "I will never leave you." Christ is a generous lover. He gave his life for us on the cross and he continues to give himself to us, especially in Holy Communion. On their wedding day, a husband and wife make a complete gift of themselves to one another, and they continue to give of themselves day in and day out throughout their marriage. Christ is a merciful lover. He redeemed us and continues to forgive our sins, especially in the Sacrament of Penance. Likewise, Christian spouses pledge to forgive one another as Christ has forgiven us. Like the two disciples whom Christ accompanied along the road to Emmaus, a Christian husband and wife who invite Christ to stay and walk with them, day by day, will experience his presence in marvelous ways. They will discover that as they draw closer to Christ, he will deepen their love for one another.

Studies have shown that married couples who attend church services regularly have stronger marriages and are less likely to divorce than those who do not do so. Even stronger and less likely to divorce are those couples who make shared prayer a regular part of their married life together. Receiving the Eucharist and the Sacrament of Penance regularly makes the self-giving love of marriage all the more possible. Thus, even in times of marital difficulty or family crisis, the grace that God makes present through prayer, worship, and participation in the sacraments will give a husband or wife the strength to pick up his or her cross and follow Christ, the perfect lover.

Questions for Reflection

1. How has your relationship been open to God's grace? Have you grown closer to one another and to Christ?

2. As a couple, do you share a vision in which God is central to your married life? Have you both come together for prayer?

3. How do your religious traditions differ? Are there any areas that need further discussion?

Communicating with God

Prayer, which is basically a conversation with God, is an important ingredient in having a fulfilling marriage and family life. Personal prayer and shared prayer between husband and wife are not only ways of strengthening a couple's relationship with God, but also with each other. Personal prayer is a conversation that can go on throughout the day. It can begin in the morning with a personal offering of the day's events, with a request for God's assistance, and with a period of reflection. It can continue throughout the day in small ways that remind us that God is present in our lives and that we act in his presence. The day can end with a review of the day and a request for God's pardon for our failings. In a like manner, shared prayer between husband and wife can be a part of these daily acts of personal prayer and can include reading the Bible or other spiritual works together, saying the Rosary together, and sharing with each other their spiritual struggles and successes.

Mixed Marriages

Today, it is common for a Catholic to marry another baptized Christian who is a non-Catholic. The Church refers to this as a mixed marriage and places great pastoral importance on helping such couples prepare for their marriage (more broadly, interreligious marriage is the term used for marriages involving a Catholic and any non-Catholic). In the Catholic Church, marriages between a Catholic and a non-Catholic require the permission of the local ecclesiastical authority. This is done in order to make sure that certain requirements are fulfilled:

• The Catholic party promises to remove dangers of falling away from the faith and to do all in his or her power to have all the children baptized and brought up in the Catholic Church;
• the non-Catholic party is to be informed of these promises; and
• must understand and intend the true meaning of married love.

These steps are not taken in order to make the process more difficult for the engaged couple but to safeguard the Catholic party's greatest possession: his or her Catholic faith. In addition, while in many cases the non-Catholic party does enter into the Church just before or soon after marriage, in those cases where the couple remains divided in their religious affiliation, difficulties often arise. In fact, these couples have a higher rate of divorce than do those in which both are Catholic.

Even though spouses in mixed marriages risk experiencing the tragedy of Christian disunity within their own homes, they also can be at the ecumenical forefront, working daily in their own marriage and family life towards that time when Christians will be divided no longer. Discovering and building upon shared values and principles, while communicating openly, honestly, and respectfully about religious differences, will contribute significantly to the harmony and happiness of a mixed marriage.

Notes

The Christian Family as the Church of the Home

For where two or three are gathered together in my name, there am I in the midst of them.
—Matthew 18:20

Christ promised his disciples that he would be with them, not only as individuals, but as a community gathered together in his name. This promise applies in a special way to the Christian family. Since the earliest centuries of the Church's existence, the Christian family has been called the "church of the home" or the "domestic church." What does this mean? Well, obviously we are not talking about the Church as a building, but rather, the Church as a place where Christ is present in a special way, a community of faith and love, like your parish, the diocese, or the universal Church. When we think of the Church in this sense, we think of a place where the Word of God is heard, where people pray, where they sincerely try to serve each other, and where they reach out to the poor and those in special need. This is also the mission of the Christian family. It is to be the first school of Christian life, where all the members help each other to grow in faith and love, living out in a privileged way the royal priesthood of Christ which we share through the Sacrament of Baptism.

Family prayer is an essential ingredient in making the Christian family the church of the home. Whether it be the family Rosary, spontaneous prayer, the Liturgy of the Hours, or simply reading from the Scriptures and meditating upon them prayerfully, what is important is that the family pray together. Pope John Paul II has written these striking words about the enduring influence of family prayer: "Only by praying together with their children can a mother and father — exercising their royal priesthood — penetrate the innermost depths of their children's hearts and leave an impression that the future events of their lives will not be able to efface." Surely the Pope, in writing these words, was reflecting in part on the lasting impression that praying together with his mother and father made on his own life. It was an impression that the future events of his life were not able to efface, for even on that fateful day in 1981 when an assassin's bullet nearly took his life, he was heard praying, even though semi-conscious and in great pain, "Mary, my mother. Mary, my mother."

Prayer to Mary, the mother of Christ, flows from the realization that Christ promised not only that he himself would be with us, but that he also gave us — as he hung on the cross — the gift of his beloved mother. She will be there for us in our family life, looking after all our needs, as she was during the wedding at Cana when the newlyweds ran out of wine. As a spouse and a mother, she understands from personal experience both the great joys and blessings of marriage and parenthood, as well as the difficulties and pain. Has any mother ever suffered as much as when she stood at the foot of the cross and saw her own divine son die a terrible death? Yet, through it all, she trusted the promise of God.

Finally, to be truly the church of the home, the Christian family cannot remain closed in on itself but must reach out in love and service to other people. In every human being, especially in the poor, the weak, those who suffer or are unjustly treated, the Christian family will know how to discover the face of Christ and will discover a fellow human being to be welcomed, loved, and served.

Ultimately, it will only be the Christian family that will, with the grace of God, be able to transform the world into a civilization of love. The future of the Church and of the world passes by way of the Christian family. Part of that future, with all its promise, will pass through your family as well.

Questions for Reflection

1. As a couple, are you both committed to building a strong family life? Have you discussed how the Catholic faith will be handed down to your children?

2. Do you both share a vision of the Christian family as the church of the home? What ideas do you have about family prayer, Scripture reading, and service to the needy among us?

3. What hopes and dreams do you have for your future family life?

Characteristics of Strong Families

Studies done on family life in various cultures throughout the world indicated that there are six qualities or characteristics that make for a strong and happy family life. These are:

1. **Commitment**. When parents are committed to each other and the family as their number one priority, their children begin to identify their membership in the family as very important. Together, the members of the family can promote a real sense of solidarity, of being all for one and one for all.

2. **Affirmation**. When parents affirm each other and each member of the family, their children begin to have a secure identity as people who are loved for who they are, and not for what talents and abilities they may have. Affirmation is an expression of an unconditional love that appreciates the person as a unique individual created in the image and likeness of God.

3. **Good Communication**. When parents communicate openly and respectfully with each other and each member of the family, their children begin to see this as a real value. Good communication means expressing oneself sincerely as well as listening attentively to the thoughts and feelings expressed by another. It involves constructive criticism that has the common good of the family as a goal.

4. **Time Investment**. When parents invest a good amount of time in their family life, family members have the opportunities to be committed, to affirm each other regularly, and to communicate effectively. The quantity and quality of time invested makes "room" for interpersonal relationships to flourish.

5. **Crisis Management**. When parents draw closer together and to their family when they are experiencing a tragedy or a difficult situation, their children learn how to overcome difficulty and even grow from it. Good crisis management depends on the qualities mentioned above as well as the qualities of confidence, courage, perseverance, and optimism. Without these qualities, families tend to fall apart rather than to experience healing.

6. **Spiritual Commitment**. When parents express their faith in God's providence, their hope in eternal life, and their love of God and neighbor, their children are raised with a solid understanding of the true meaning of life. An active spiritual life will give members of the family the virtues they need to resist destructive behaviors, to overcome difficulties, and to lead good and productive lives. It is the only sure path to real happiness.

NOTES